Ahmad Abu Zannad is a brand marketing and advertising strategist who worked for Leo Burnett and Zain for over 17 years. He has been fortunate to get acquainted with consumers from different backgrounds, businesses operating in a multitude of industries and talent with diverse skillsets. As an avid reader, Ahmad's passion is to showcase the application of what he reads into his work.

Back in 2012, he wrote his first book on the Saudi market, predicting most of the transformation that the market has been witnessing. Then his second book in 2016 was on the de-commoditization of the ad industry.

Ahmad is currently the founder and lead strategist at Native Communications, an advisory firm dedicated to ensuring that brands and their ads play a 'native' role in people's lives.

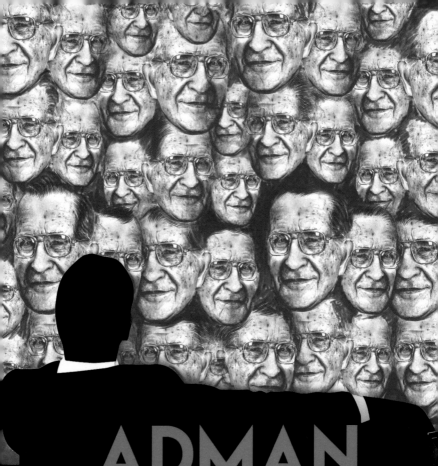

ADMAN VS. CHOMSKY

AHMAD ABU ZANNAD

CHALLENGING CHOMSKY'S STATEMENT

"The advertising industry's prime task is to ensure that uninformed consumers make irrational choices."

AUSTIN MACAULEY PUBLISHERS™
LONDON • CAMBRIDGE • NEW YORK • SHARJAH

ISBN – 9789948844907 – (Paperback)
ISBN – 9789948844891 – (E-Book)

Application Number: MC-10-01-1036374
Age Classification: E

Printer Name: iPrint Global Ltd
Printer Address: Witchford, England

First Published (2021)
AUSTIN MACAULEY PUBLISHERS FZE
Sharjah Publishing City
P.O Box [519201]
Sharjah, UAE
www.austinmacauley.ae
+971 655 95 202

To my late father. Thank you for your endless belief that somehow, someday, I will venture into something ambitious and see it all the way through. This is what drove me to finally finish this book.

TABLE OF CONTENTS

CHAPTER I

THE AD INDUSTRY'S IMAGE PROBLEM AND THE NEED TO TAKE ON THE MOST INTELLECTUAL HUMAN ALIVE

"I would say the days of advertising
as we know it today are numbered,
and we need to start thinking about
a world with no ads."

—

*M*arc *P*ritchard
CHIEF BRAND OFFICER OF P&G

In January 2019, the Chief Brand Officer of P&G, one of the world's biggest advertisers, made headlines for a statement he made at CES 2019, an event held by the Consumer Technology Association in Las Vegas. "I would say the days of advertising as we know it today are numbered, and we need to start thinking about a world with no ads," Marc Pritchard declared.

While the rest of his talk showcased some of P&G's recent product innovations that allow for at-scale personalization and a direct link between brands and their consumers, in no way was Pritchard calling for a future with absolutely no ads. However, what was revealing and eye-opening about his comments was the earth-shattering reaction to the headline, "P&G's Top Marketer is Predicting a World with No Ads." People from the ad industry freaked out, consumers were almost relieved, while other clients aspired to follow in Pritchard's footsteps.

This and other recent events have raised the big question:

HAS THE CREATIVE AD INDUSTRY LOST ITS MOJO?

This and other recent events have raised the big question: Has the creative ad industry lost its mojo? An old-timer from the industry once told me how his clients would wait for people from the agency to visit their offices, just to catch a look at what new trendy fashions the "mad men" would be wearing, and what kind of show they might put on. Clients would anxiously wait to hear about their latest adventures, or even seek their advice on the new popular outings. Yes, believe it or not, there was a time when clients didn't just admire their agency and the individuals who worked there - they were fascinated by them. This went beyond their love for the agency's work for them, because such love would certainly have its ups and downs; instead, it was a consistently fruitful partnership that, from the client's end, was based on awe and respect, and, from the agency's end, was based on the passion to create ideas that drive their clients' business.

It is not just the client's admiration that has slipped since the glory days of advertising. As Andrew Cracknell explains in *The Real Mad Men: The Remarkable True Story of Madison Avenue's Golden Age*, there was a time when top talent longed to work in the industry. People in advertising were passionately in love with their jobs and felt they were the masters of their own domain. In fact, they were the envy of almost everyone in business, as their work was seen as having the highest level of charm. Even audiences would eagerly look forward to creative ads which, in the late 1960s and early 1970s, were a driving force behind the era's popular culture.

I have felt some of these shifts firsthand in my own career. Less than 10 years ago, when I was heading a marketing unit at the client's end, I clearly recall that, out of all the different phases of a marketing project, the work with the agency was the most enjoyable.

Back then, to me, every launch of a marketing value proposition felt like the plot to a Mission Impossible-style movie:

It always started with our unrealistic and impossible targets; in a voice similar to that of Anthony Hopkins, the CEO would tell us that we somehow had to double our profits from the previous year. This is the part of the plot where Tom Cruise would get the message that would self-destruct in five seconds (and, in my head, I'd be hoping that I was Cruise and that the CEO was somehow about to self-destruct). Then my Mission Impossible began, as I assembled my team. In the movie version, this is where Cruise would bring in his computer geeks (i.e., my data and marketing research analysts) to discuss highly classified files (i.e., the consumer), how to infiltrate the secured location (i.e., the market) and how to overcome, beat, or kill the bad guys (i.e., the competition).

From there, I would strategize and explore our own capabilities to identify and develop value propositions, products, services, platforms, retail outlets, touch points, and experiences to help us achieve our targets. Here is where things get boring; the audience would just be left hanging in there, waiting for the action to begin, as I undertook pricing battles with finance, lobbying for regulatory approvals, and lots of endlessly dull meetings with sales, customer care, product development, etc.

16

BUT THEN!

But then! Things start heating up when it's time for the briefing to my communication agency. This is the part of the story where the hero hooks up with the fast-talking, good-looking partner, and, just like that, the film has gotten much more interesting. Once the agency started coming back to me with its creative ideas, I felt like I was falling in love with my own creation all over again.

There were dazzling agency presentations, boasting the same hyped-up energy as a scene where the partner is all dressed up at some gala dinner, pulling all sorts of creative tricks to help the hero in his mission. And, once the campaign was launched (and that part of the mission turned out to be possible after all), I felt not just a sense of pride in the work, but also intense admiration for the work of my communication agency - it was like the big Hollywood ending, where Cruise is running towards his partner for that one final embrace.

Client

Agency

So, during my own experience as a marketer, working with the advertising agency was practically the only charming, exciting, and interesting part of an overall marketing project. Yet, today, when I talk to my fellow marketers, they no longer see it that way. For them, it has become the meetings with the Googles, Facebooks, and Snapchats of the world that steal the show. The agencies have been demoted, from costars to unimportant side characters.

As an industry, we may have lost our mojo; however, this book is neither a reminiscence on the history of the industry, nor is it another think piece on its future, of which there are now far more than enough (considering that a Google search for "the future of the advertising industry" returns 600 million results and counting). I am personally among those who have been attempting to strategically recommend where the industry ought to be heading, having written a book and numerous articles on the subject - but again, this is not one of them. Instead, this book is actually a defense of the industry as it has stood in its recent history and as it stands today. In fact, I will argue that there has been a severe misunderstanding of what the ad industry is all about.

This misunderstanding has caused great harm to the industry, particularly as clients have stopped viewing us in the same manner. In 2015, IPA Client Relationship Group commissioned Hall & Partners to explore the state of the client-agency relationship. Their conclusion was basically that it is in *crisis*. From the clients' end, the key takeaways were that agencies were not understanding their world, not understanding their customers, or not keeping pace with the latest innovations and technologies.[1]

However, from the agency side, one main issue was almost unanimously raised:

Clients do not value us as much as they once did. Our relationships are weaker, shorter, and include more and more pitching.

The negative effects of the crisis in the industry are already being felt. Unilever, a major client, has decided to cut its agencies in half, according to a June 2017 statement by its Chief Marketing and Communications Officer, Keith Weed, who also stated that they will cut the number of ads they're running by 30%. Also, in November 2016, P&G announced

---

There is merit to all these complaints; yet, as mentioned earlier, these are topics that have been overly discussed in other venues. In this book, we are more concerned with the observations coming from the agency side of the very same report.

that it will cut its agencies by almost 50%. Even earlier, in October 2015, Brad Jakeman, PepsiCo's president of global beverage group, expressed his dissatisfaction with agencies, leveling harsh accusations that "agencies aren't pulling their weight" and that "they need to either catch up with current trends or get dumped." (We'll have to get back to whether or not Mr. Jakeman's idea of salvaging the issue was producing the company's infamous Kendall Jenner ad using in-house creatives).

Agency

Client

To add insult to injury, our perception problem is not just affecting our relationship with clients - it is also coming from within the core of our offering: our talent. Creatives today are becoming much less interested in joining our field. According to the Wall Street Journal, the advertising industry loses more jobs and talent than any other, having shed 65% of all jobs over the past decade. Meanwhile, employee recruitment and retention are estimated to have costed the advertising and media industry a staggering £184m per year, according to a 2014 IPA report.

And, worst of all, even our owners - the major holding companies - have been undermining the value of their creative agencies by constantly undercutting investments into them. In his book *Madison Avenue Manslaughter: An Inside View of Fee-cutting Clients, Profit-Hungry Owners and Declining Ad Agencies*, Michael Farmer shows how the capabilities of creative agencies have been diminishing due to underinvestment by their holding companies.

In a nutshell, internally, we are losing our bloodline -
we are a talent-based industry losing a high number
of talent. Consequently, our capabilities are being
diminished. At the same time, externally, we are losing
our lifeline - we can only live through our clients,
and the most sophisticated marketers among them
no longer believe in our value and are constantly
attempting to slash our fees . Finally, our owners have
been underinvesting in us, believing that future growth
will only come from investments in technology firms,
consequently, our capabilities are being diminished.

[2] One might argue that clients are experiencing economic crisis and are simply trying to
cut costs. But when financials are tight, the first thing you get rid of is the fat, and as
an industry, we cannot afford to be seen as the fat. Also, as Henry Ford said, 'Stopping
advertising to save money is like stopping your watch to save time.'

So why is this happening? And what can be done about it? Well, a main reason behind the aforementioned negative state of the industry is the fact that we have been passively losing almost every intellectual conversation around our possible positive contributions. Key among these intellectual conversations have been initiated by perhaps the most intellectual human alive, American linguist, philosopher, academic, and political theorist Dr. Noam Chomsky, who argues that

" THE PRIME TASK OF THE ADVERTISING INDUSTRY IS TO ENSURE UNINFORMED CONSUMERS MAKE IRRATIONAL CHOICES. "

—

NOAM CHOMSKY

Judging by the state of the industry, there is certainly a need for someone to defend what advertising is about - even if that does mean going after and debating one of the world's leading thinkers. Because, more than ever, there is an existential need for a solid intellectual argument relaying the potential positive contributions of this industry, not only for the businesses of its clients, but for the overall economy on a macro level, and for the wellbeing of the human race on a personal level. This book is an initial attempt to do so. It is a stand for the hardworking admen and women, and an effort to attract and retain top talent as well as to give the industry its bloodline back.

It is a showcase to the world's holding companies of the potential value of their creative agencies, and proof of the need for them to start re-investing in their capabilities. Finally, it is an effort to prove to clients that we are not only essential for their brands, but for the survival of their businesses, so that we may regain our premium position and give our beloved industry its lifeline back.

In order to do so, the structure of the book is a breakdown of Chomsky's aforementioned statement:

DISSECTING CHOMSKY'S STATEMENT

"THE PRIME TASK OF THE ADVERTISING INDUSTRY IS TO ENSURE UNINFORMED CONSUMERS MAKE IRRATIONAL CHOICES."

It dissects the statement and attempts to argue against each of its points, beginning with the notion that it is our "prime task" to do what he accused us of, and proving the same could be said of the most noble of industries, including those in medicine and even of those in Chomsky's field of education. Yes, it is possible to take the extreme worst-case scenario of industry practitioners utilizing their skillsets to persuade uninformed consumers to make irrational choices, and label it as their prime task, in any industry.

Then, the book introduces the reader to the group of human beings whom Chomsky referred to as the "uninformed," using findings from other scientific fields (such as behavioral economics) to make the point that it is not the ad industry's fault that the uniformed will almost always remain uninformed. On the contrary, it is the ad industry that has been and will be the salvation of our economic systems from possible collapse, despite this scientific fact. After that, it takes a look at "irrational choices," demonstrating that the human nature to make irrational choices is not the result of advertising, nor is taking advantage of this instinct a prime task of the industry.

In fact, based on scientific evidence from the fields of psychology, evolutionary psychology, and behavioral economics, the industry's efforts to persuade people to make irrational choices is a result of this human nature, and not the cause.

To shed light on a more positive definition of the task of the advertising industry, the book brings to the surface the potential essentiality of the ad industry for the wellbeing of the entire human race, backing this argument up with scientific experiments and actual case studies on showing that, when practiced purposefully, advertising can be crucial. Finally, it proposes an alternative definition to Chomsky's description of the prime task of the advertising industry.

CHAPTER II

"THE UNINFORMED": HOW ADVERTISING CAN SAVE ECONOMIES, DESPITE MARKET THEORIES

"Advertising may convey no information
other than that the firm can afford to
advertise, but that may be all a consumer
needs to know to have confidence in it."

—

The Economist

Adam Smith

If we were to look at the entirety of Chomsky?s statement that we are challenging, the remainder goes as follows:

: "The advertising industry's prime task is to ensure that uninformed consumers make irrational choices, *thus undermining market theories that are based on just the opposite.*"

Accordingly, the question that comes to mind is, what are the market theories Chomsky is accusing the advertising industry of undermining? And is the advertising industry in fact doing so? To answer this, we must go back to the very theories to which Chomsky is referring, in order to reveal that they have been subverted not by advertising, but due to their actual application in the real world.

Our economic systems and free markets are almost all based on Adam Smith's invisible hand theory. The theory states that if governments leave buyers and sellers to freely make their decisions, buyers will only pay the price they see fit for products and services, while sellers will, in turn, only sell for the price that they see fit. When this buyer-seller perfectly rational behavior is present with free trade and open competition, the market reaches its optimal price, helped along by the invisible hand.

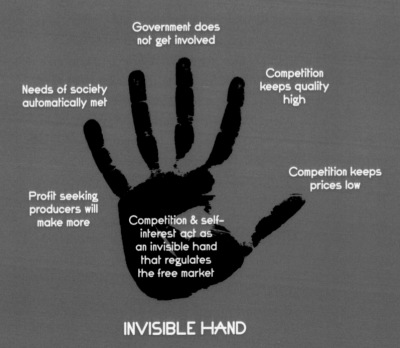

Government does
not get involved

Competition
keeps quality
high

Needs of society
automatically met

Competition keeps
prices low

Profit seeking
producers will
make more

Competition & self-
interest act as
an invisible hand
that regulates
the free market

INVISIBLE HAND

However, there are abnormalities and exceptions that, in practice, have proven that the theory is not always accurate. For some, the solution has been resorting to government interventions, such as when the seller has a monopoly over the market, or when there's a third party, like the environment, being affected.

Another exception occurs in cases of what economists refer to as asymmetry of information - when either the seller or the buyer possesses information about what is being sold that the other does not. Such an exception could possibly push markets to fail. 2001 Nobel Memorial Prize in Economic Sciences recipient, George Akerlof, was the first to discuss the negative consequences of information asymmetry in his 1970 paper "The Market for Lemons: Quality Uncertainty and the Market Mechanism." His paper presented the case of when only the seller has the information needed to differentiate between a lemon - American slang for a defective used car - and a peach - a high-quality one.

His hypothesis was that buyers who cannot tell the difference between a lemon and a peach will be unwilling to pay the full price of a peach, as they are unsure of its quality, while for sellers, selling a peach will no longer be in their best interest as there are no buyers willing to pay for it. Accordingly, the used car market ought to include only defective cars, and would eventually collapse.

MARKET FAILURE: ASYMMETRIC INFORMATION (AKERLOF'S LEMONS)

BUYER

SELLER

- Unsure which car is which
- Will buy if value > = price
- Will only take the chance and pay $2,500

....

- Low quality
- Worth $1,000

- Sure which car is which
- Will sell if price >= value
- Has no interest in selling a peach for $2,500
- Ends up only selling lemons

....

- High quality
- Worth $4,000

Asymmetry of information relates to the individuals Chomsky referred to as "the uninformed," or the buyers who lack the ability or motivation to tell if the product or service they are about to purchase is of good quality. Neuro-marketer Martin Lindstrom's massive Functional MRI study showed that 90 percent of purchase decisions are made subconsciously. As he explains, in today's world, we make almost 10,000 decisions a day, most of which have to do with buying something. Accordingly, there's almost no way we'd have the capacity to be well-informed about all of these purchase decisions.

FUNCTIONAL MRI

REVEALED THAT 90% OF PURCHASE DECISIONS ARE MADE SUBCONSCIOUSLY

So, if we accept that 90 percent of buying decisions are made with asymmetry of information, and, if we were to apply Akerlof's "market for lemons" hypothesis, then an assumption could be made that 90 percent of marketplace offerings are of defective quality - and that 90 percent of industries are doomed to collapse! So why haven't they? Advertising and brand building.

Written in 1759, Adam Smith?s theory was put to the test post the first industrial revolution, which started around the same period (1760) and lasted until around the 1830s. The industrial revolution allowed for suppliers, manufactures, engineers, inventors, and eventually sellers to produce on a mass scale, which propelled them to distribute and sell to a wider buyers' base (or customer base) in different geographies. This meant that the distance between sellers and buyers was growing further, pushing buyers to buy from sellers they had no idea who they were, what was their background, where their facilities were, what were their values etc....

which meant buyers had no guarantee on the quality of the products they wanted to buy. Such information asymmetry on such a massive scale should have meant that markets would fail, since buyers would not be willing to buy the full price of the products, and sellers would not be able to afford to sell their good quality products at the prices the buyers were suggesting.

Yet, with manufacturing at such massive scale, came branding and advertising at a similar massive scale. It was not a coincidence that around that same period advertising officially became a profession, with the first ad agency being established in 1786 by William Taylor in London.

Then came even more advancements in distribution with massive construction of railways and sea routes, widening the gap between sellers and buyers even further. This was during the second half of the nineteenth century, and gave birth to more brands with mass appeal, including Levi's in 1850, Tabasco in 1868, Heinz in 1869, Pure Honey Soap in 1874 (Unilever today), Ivory Soap in 1879 (P&G today), Coca-Cola in 1886, Pepsi-Cola in 1898, Kodak in 1887, and Philips in 1891.

As we can see above, it hasn't taken long for economists to come to the realization that adverting and brand building make the world easier and less stressful to navigate. For instance, no matter where in the world you might be, iconic brands such as Coca-Cola and McDonald's have made your purchase decisions not only easier and less stressful, but also joyful. After all, there's nothing better and simpler than an airport Big Mac! As such, it is safe to state that advertising and brand building are out there ensuring that markets do not fail in the face of overwhelming information asymmetry.

Information asymmetry is an exception proving that basic market theories, such as free markets, are not 100 percent applicable as is in the actual marketplace - these are the very same market theories Chomsky accused the advertising industry of undermining. But in reality, we can make the case that advertising and brand building have helped us overcome the negative consequences of such common exceptions.

What we are referring to as adverting and brand building is what other Economics Nobel Prize recipients refer to as "signaling." Michael Spence of Stanford University and Joseph Stiglitz of Columbia have collaborated to showcase the applications of signaling in the job market. According to them, employers looking to hire job applicants have asymmetry of information in regards to the capabilities and skillsets of the applicants. Accordingly, job applicants invest heavily in signals that will help them stand out from the competition, in the form of paying very high premiums to attend prestigious universities. The more difficult it is to attend such universities, the more attractive these applicants become, even though such an education is often irrelevant to the job they are applying for.

In the extreme worst-case scenario, advertisers take advantage of buyers? ignorance, aiming to persuade ?the uninformed? to make irrational choices and be overcharged for goods they do not need. Yet it is unfair and unrealistic to label this deception as the prime task of the entire advertising industry. After all, there are many instances where advertising and brand building have been crucial in salvaging markets on the verge of collapsing under the burden of asymmetry of information.

Carmakers, tech innovators, FMCG manufacturers, and service providers such as airlines, banks, and telecom operators would not be able to afford to provide high-quality offerings if their consumers were unwilling to pay their products' full price - and without sufficient information (in the constant absence of consumers' motivation and/or ability to attain such information), consumers would have probably refused. It was the advertisers and brand builders who created signals of reassurances, inspiring people's trust and love for brands like Apple, Samsung, Mercedes, Emirates Airlines, McDonald's, and Dove.

42

Brands like these ensure that people who lack the ability or motivation to look into the caliber of their products will still agree to pay their full price; this has allowed these sellers to invest in the quality of what they are providing, thereby keeping their markets afloat.

This could be perceived as an extremely idealistic view of advertising and brand building, especially as, very often, advertising uses people's love and trust for their brands as an excuse to charge them more than a product is actually worth. However, while the ad industry creates signals of love and trust, it is not the industry responsible for abusing uninformed consumers - that blame resides squarely on the shoulders of deceptive clients. At the same time, it is a fact that advertising and brand building have massively contributed to the aforementioned achievements.

Finally, this very same accusation that has been levelled against advertising could also be applied to an industry like education. Chomsky, for example, is employed at MIT, one of the most expensive academic institutions in the world, with an average annual tuition fee of over $41,500. The U.S. National Inflation Association (NIA) has noted that no industry has seen more consistent price inflation during the past decade than college education. And, according to PBS' Hari Sreenivasan, college student loan debt in the U.S. now stands at $1.4 trillion - higher than what Americans owe on their credit cards or car loans. In fact, the NIA estimated that two-thirds of college students now graduate with an average of $24,000 in debt.

Despite skyrocketing inflation and tuition debt, at the moment, higher education is not necessarily helping people find jobs like it used to. A 2015 survey of 30,000 alumni, conducted by Gallup-Purdue Index, showed that only 38 percent of students who have graduated college in the past decade strongly agree that their higher education was worth the cost. Would freshman students still agree to pay these rising tuitions if they knew that the return on their investment might not be all they've been led to believe? Or are colleges taking advantage of young people's ignorance?

ONLY 38 PERCENT OF STUDENTS WHO HAVE GRADUATED COLLEGE IN THE PAST DECADE STRONGLY AGREE THAT THEIR HIGHER EDUCATION WAS WORTH THE COST.

38%

Furthermore, the very same accusation could be levelled at those in what might be perceived as the most noble of professions, medical doctors. There is no doubt that those who have dedicated their lives to healing others are like angels, working day in and day out to save lives. However, there are many instances where they also ensure that "uniformed" patients (or consumers of their services) make irrational choices. In fact, Fransisco Contreras' *Health in the 21st Century* shows that, in the U.S alone, an estimated 7.5 million unnecessary medical and surgical procedures are performed annually, while there are 8.9 million unnecessary hospital stays.

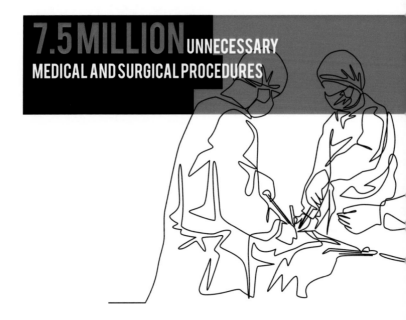

7.5 MILLION UNNECESSARY MEDICAL AND SURGICAL PROCEDURES

In today's markets, asymmetry of information is an unavoidable fact. But while many practitioners often utilize their skillsets to take advantage of it, it is still unfair to declare this practice the prime task of entire industries. If we were to do so of the advertising industry, then we could also do the same with the education and healthcare industries. Would we be justified to make the statement that the main goal of academic institutions is to ensure that students pay unjustifiably high premiums for unnecessary education, in the hope that uninformed employers might possibly make the irrational choice of hiring them? Or could we define the prime task of medical doctors as one to ensure that uniformed patients make the irrational choice of paying for unnecessary procedures?

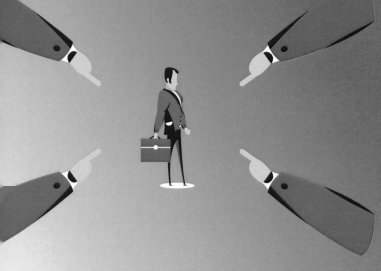

If not, we must recognize that there are nuances to the three industries; education, medicine, and advertising. To brand any of them as black or white would be very simplistic - it would be more accurate and productive to look deeper, into the shades of gray.

As for the market theories Chomsky accused the advertising industry of undermining, information asymmetry is only one of many exceptions proving that the wholesale application of these theories is unworkable in real life. Applying them exactly as they appear on paper could have caused markets to collapse; in the instance of information asymmetry, it took advertising and brand building to help markets overcome such a consequence. Therefore, the notion that advertising is somehow only after "the uninformed" cannot be reconciled with the realities of the marketplace. In the next chapter, we will challenge Chomsky's reference to "irrational choices" and explore just how illogical our brains can sometimes be.

CHAPTER III

IRRATIONAL CHOICES

UNDERSTANDING ILLOGICAL CONSUMER BEHAVIOR

"Thinking is to humans as swimming
is to cats; they can do it but they'd
prefer not to."

—

Daniel Kahneman

In the previous chapter the discussion was around the challenge that was set forward against classical economics theory which proposes that at any moment in time where a transaction is taking place, both sellers and buyers are constantly equipped with perfect information. The challenge was set through the concept of asymmetry of information along with the Lemon Dilemma and the market for used cars.

During the endeavor we met Noble prize recipients in economics theory such as George Akerlof, Michael Spence and Joseph Stiglitz to prove the point that while asymmetry of information could have possibly caused markets to fail, it was what economists refer to as the signaling theory that was there for the rescue, and at a wider space beyond the job market, signaling comes in the form of advertising and brand building, to conclude that the latter two could have potentially been the salvation of free markets.

In this chapter, another assumption of classic economics will be challenged, and that is the fact that humans in the marketplace will constantly act in a rational manner, or what traditional economists refer to as 'Rational Choice Model'; taking this back to Chomsky's accusation of the ad industry as the primary force behind people's irrational choices in the marketplace.

CHALLENGING THE RATIONAL CHOICE THEORY

Rational Choice Theory says we make rational, utility-maximizing decisions, and that's not true:

——

1. In commerce we don't have all the information we would need to make the best possible decision

——

2. Confirmation bias, Selective Perception, and Optical Illusions are often the drivers, not logic or reason

——

3. Commerce is more like a card game with hidden information, than a chess game where there is no hidden information

Lecture by Ira Gorelick 'Rationality and Commerce'. March 2015

To do so, concepts and thoughts from a relatively new economics field will be borrowed, that field is behavioral economics. In addition, another two Noble prize recipients will be introduced, they are Richard H. Thaler and Daniel Kahneman (both considered to be the founding fathers of behavioral economics).

Behavioral economics emerged to shed light into a more human side to decision making, it did so by marrying the science of psychology with economics. As such, its premise revolves around the fact that in the absence of perfect information, humans tend to rarely make flawlessly rational choices; on the contrary, humans will tend to mostly make irrational choices, while such choices often may not be in their best interest.

CLASSICAL ECONOMICS   VS   BEHAVIORAL ECONOMICS

—

Economists design their models assuming people are perfectly rational and predictable: homo economicus attempt to maximize their utility in all instances

—

Behavioral economists do not subscribe to rational choice theory, they believe individuals make irrational decisions and explore dynamics thereof

Jacob Reynolds. Behavioural Economics: making a case against rational choice theory.

The more behavioral economists attempted to unearth human insights around decision making; and the more they have experimented with the application of psychology into the field of economics, the more they found a big dichotomy between the humans traditional economists threw into their assumptions and the actual humans they were meeting. According to Daniel Kahneman,

ECONS

' WELL-DEFINED PREFERENCES
' DECISIONS MAXIMIZE ALL ALTERNATIVES
' MAKES RATIONAL ACTIONS
' PURSUES MONETARY GAIN

HUMANS

' PREFERENCES LESS DEFINED
' EASIEST PATH IS OFTEN THE CHOICE
' VULNERABLE TO GUILT, FAIRNESS, SOCIAL COMPARISON, DESIRE FOR LUXURY

ConversationAgent.com

in his book Thinking, Fast and Slow: "it seems that traditional economics and behavioral economics are describing two different species." While, Richard H. Thaler, in his book Misbehaving had a more elaborate description of the humans traditional economists refer to, he calls these fictional creatures "Econs," as in, they only exist in the world of economic theories. Now, to better understand the application of psychology into humans' decision making, we need to better understand how humans process information prior to making any decision, and we can do so through psychology's Dual Process Theory. The Dual Process Theory states that when people process information, they use either one of two routes:

i.   The Peripheral Route: this uses the S1 part of the brain, which is 'old' from an evolutionary perspective. The manner in which information is processed in this system is very instinctive, impulsive, emotional, and intuitive (i.e., it is not necessarily very rational).

ii.   The Central Route: this uses the S2 part
of the brain, which is far more recent from an
evolutionary standpoint; it is here that information
is processed in a rational, logical, conscious, and
reflective manner.

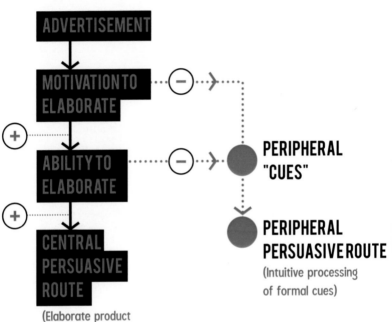

The Essence of ELM

The theory also states that the route for processing information is determined by two factors: Motivation and Ability. When people lack these two factors (i.e., the case of asymmetry of information), they process information through the Peripheral Route. If these two factors are present when processing information, then they use the Central Route.

If we go back to Neuro-marketing, and the study showcasing that 90% of purchase decisions are made subconsciously (i.e., through S1 part of the brain, and/or irrationally), again according to Lindstorm, with 10,000 decisions to make per day, people rarely have the motivation or ability to process the information about the products and services they are about to purchase. Also, it is not only about the massive number of choices humans have to make per day, according to Kahneman, while the human brain is only 2 percent of their total body weight,

"Thinking is to humans as swimming is to cats; they can do it, but they'd prefer not to."

it demands 20 percent of their resting metabolic rate (RMR), accordingly we have evolved the mechanism to use our brains as less as possible; as a survival technique to save as much of our energy as possible. In his own words, Kahneman states: "Thinking is to humans as swimming is to cats; they can do it but they'd prefer not to."

Therefore, with asymmetry of information being a fact of nature, along with people's constant lack of motivation and/or ability to process information about a product or a service, meaning that people will end up using S1 part of their brain (i.e., making irrational purchase decisions), the questions that need to be answered here are:

Questions:

1. SHOULD ENSURING THAT UNIFORMED CONSUMERS ARE INFORMED BE THE PRIMARY TASK OF ADVERTISING? IS ADVERTISING SOMEHOW HIDING INFORMATION AWAY FROM CONSUMERS TO ENSURE THEY MAKE IRRATIONAL CHOICES?

Answers:

1. To this question we need to point out that there was indeed a point in time where advertisers might have enjoyed an information advantage over consumers, as in they knew more about the product and/or service while being selective in what information to reveal and what to not to reveal. Today, this is definitely no longer the case since any consumer who is willing and able to attain such information has an abundance of sources to get this information. In fact, it is the ongoing challenge for advertisers to get people interested enough in what is being advertised to start seeking such information,

there is also the nature of the category for what is being advertised.

Often the nature of such categories is what is referred to as "low involvement categories."

An abundance of consumer reviews

This means that given the nature of the product and/or service consumers tend to be unmotivated to get involved in features/ qualities/attributes of what they are about to buy; think about buying chewing gum, underwear, instant coffee etc....

although it is unfair to give specific examples here, for this strictly depends on the character of the consumer.

I mean while I personally might be constantly unmotivated to seek information on the quality of the chewing gum I'm about to buy, there might be people out there obsessed with chewing gum: the richness of its flavor, how refreshing it is, how chewy, the size of the bubble it helps them blow, and I'm honestly unsure what other information these chewing gum freaks might want to seek. In conclusion, the answer to the first part of the question is YES, advertising should seek to ensure that uninformed consumers are informed, however, the fact that they are often still uninformed is no shortcoming of advertising. The fact is from an advertising information processing science perspective, when dealing with motivated and capable consumers (i.e., individuals "thinking slowly," using S2 part of their brain and making rational choices) we have developed a suite of tools and frameworks for the delivery of the message to be as efficient and effective as possible, making the lives of such consumers as easy as possible. Key among such tool is the Means-End-Chain (MEC) Model (please refer to figure X for more details on the MEC model). The on-going challenge for advertisers have been to be this efficient and effective when having to deal with uninformed consumers making irrational choices, and while we think we have cracked the code for one type of decision making, we really have not done so yet for the second type

[3] Another relatively recent scientific field, evolutionary psychology, helps us address irrational behavior, and its application in advertising will be discussed in further details in Chapter 4.

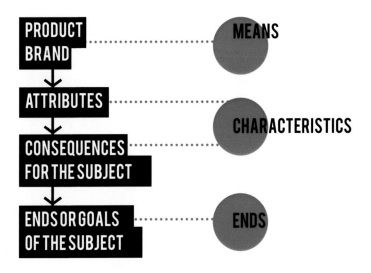

PRODUCT BRAND .... MEANS

ATTRIBUTES ....

CONSEQUENCES FOR THE SUBJECT .... CHARACTERISTICS

ENDS OR GOALS OF THE SUBJECT .... ENDS

This brings us to another pressing question:

SHOULD THE AD INDUSTRY ALONE BE HELD ACCOUNTABLE FOR TAKING ADVANTAGE OF THE IRRATIONAL CHOICES OF UNINFORMED CONSUMERS?

The answer to this query is simply 'no'. First of all, informing consumers is a shared responsibility, most of which lies on the shoulders of suppliers.

As for the second part of the same question. Well, there might have been a point in time where advertisers enjoyed the luxury of hiding information, however, we just passed the information age, and for any consumer willing to attain any information about any product and/or service, there are more than enough sources available for literally anyone, and such information is articulated in the simplest of formats (like user reviews) which overcomes the 'ability' constraint.

2. Is taking advantage of the irrational choices made by uninformed consumers the sole responsibility of the ad industry?

The answer to the second question is simply **NO**. It is a shared responsibility with more weight to be on the shoulders of suppliers.

In fact, while the ad industry, as many other industries, might have taken advantage of people's tendency to make irrational choices, there are many instances where it took advertising to persuade the uninformed-irrational-decision-makers to make choices that have benefited these peoples' economies. For example, when Frederick the Great, of Prussia, was faced by an economic harsh reality during the 1700s: his people might start dying from hunger, unless they start massively farming potatoes, however, his people (uninformed and behaving irrationally) refused to plant potatoes, because they simply perceived them as ugly and as the food for the less fortunate. Frederick realized that in order to solve this issue, his only solution was to build the potato brand, accordingly, he announced that potato is an exclusive luxury that only the royal were able to grow in their gardens, and he had potato gardens get fulltime protection by the royal guards. In reaction, his irrational people grew madly obsessed with potato, they started growing their own underground potato farms, and because of the fact that they did so, the economy had been salvaged. So, here's another example of how advertising and brand building can potentially salvage markets and economies.

In conclusion, people will continue making their irrational choices irrespective of advertising, yet in an open economy such irrational choices may cause markets to collapse.

Again, it takes advertising and brand building to build a trusting relationship between sellers and uninformed-irrational buyers.

Frederick the Great

Advertising should not be defined as the business persuading people to make irrational choices, even at the instances where it is felt that these irrational choices are obviously the results of an ad. Such instances and the deeper reasons behind them will be discussed in the next chapter.

CHAPTER IV

ADVERTISING'S REAL RELATIONSHIP WITH IRRATIONAL CHOICES

"Had marketers and advertisers been able to socialize the human brain into the irrational decisions it has been making in the marketplace then we would have had the near-infinite ability to socialize consumers into endless new patterns of consumption."

———

Gad Saad

Evolutionary
Psychologist

Are the irrational choices consumers making the result of advertising (examples: buying overpriced flashy items, obsession with sex, and/or consuming fatty unhealthy food)?

Observing the marketplace, one cannot help but notice the various irrational choices people have been making, key among them will be the following:

i) **O**verpaying for flashy items: the price for McLaren, Paintings, Wine, Handbags, watches etc.

ii) **O**bsession with sex and physical appearance: consumption of adult content (there are 2.5 billion emails containing adult content being sent or received), sexy lingerie, beauty products, plastic surgery.

iii) Consumption of unhealthy fatty food and confectionaries: **Fast-food chains selling fatty food are the top revenue generating food suppliers, the Atkins diet craze etc.**

The above brings us to the question:

HAS THIS BEEN THE OUTCOME OF MARKETING AND ADVERTISING TAKING ADVANTAGE OF PEOPLE'S IRRATIONALITY?

To answer this, we need to better understand how a human's evolutionary old brain functions, and fortunately, we can do so, through the science of Evolutionary Psychology (EP).

During the exploration of the application of EP into the fields of marketing and advertising, we will get acquainted with two prominent academics and published authors who have been the driving force behind these applications, Gad Saad (my charismatic consumer behavior professor from my university years and author of the book: *The Consuming Instinct: What Juicy Burgers, Ferraris, Pornography and Gift Giving Reveal About Human Nature*) and Geoffrey Miller (author of the book: *Spent: Sex, Evolution, and Consumer Behavior*). Just as evolutionary biology explains how our organic parts have specific functions based on adaptations through the processes of natural selection and sexual selection*, EP explains how certain human behaviors were shaped as a result of similar adaptations. Accordingly, the first scientific challenge EP puts on the table goes for social sciences and their blank-slate view of the human mind, which assumes that as humans we are born with empty minds that are eventually socialized into what we are to become through a variety of environmental factors (examples: family, friends, films, videos, and based on the topic of this book there is also advertising).

*According to Darwin: "The sexual struggle is of two kinds; in the one it is between individuals of the same sex, generally the males, in order to drive away or kill their rivals, the females remaining passive; whilst in the other, the struggle is likewise between the individuals of the same sex, in order to excite or charm those of the opposite sex, generally the females, which no longer remain passive, but select the more agreeable partners."

Challenging the blank-slate view, evolutionary psychology shows us that we aren't born with empty minds that are eventually filled through socialization. Alternatively, as humans we are born with innate biological blueprints.

THE BLANK-SLATE THEORY:

Examples given by evolutionary psychologists will include the reason why a 3-month-old baby stares at a beautiful face longer than a non-beautiful face,

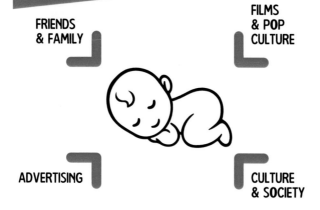

FRIENDS
& FAMILY

FILMS
& POP
CULTURE

ADVERTISING

CULTURE
& SOCIETY

babies do this without being inducted on what defines beauty. This does not suggest that, as humans (or consumers) we are strictly the product of our innate biological blue print, what defines our behavior is a mix of our environment (including our social and cultural upbringing) and our biology. Yet as consumers, biology and our innate biological blueprint are more influential to our decision making when we are using our S1 part of the brain. Again, this is a part of the brain that is acting instinctively, impulsively, and most importantly irrationally.

Therefore, for such purchase decisions and for such consumer behavior, marketing and advertising are in no way the cause of the behavior.

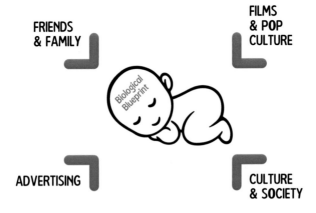

FRIENDS & FAMILY

FILMS & POP CULTURE

Biological Blueprint

ADVERTISING

CULTURE & SOCIETY

If anything, marketing and advertising are only reacting and/or catering for this pre-existing behavior. According to Gad Saad, had marketers and advertisers been able to socialize the human brain into the irrational decisions it has been making in the marketplace then we would have had "the near-infinite ability to socialize consumers into endless new patterns of consumption." EP has brought with it lots of evidence on how most of the choices we make as humans and subsequently as consumers are the results of our evolutionary past, as the evolutionary geneticist Theodosius Dobzhansky once stated: "Nothing in biology makes sense except in the light of evolution," Gad Saad, the evolutionary psychologist will argue: "Nothing in consumer behavior makes sense except in the light of evolution."

"NOTHING IN CONSUMER BEHAVIOR MAKES SENSE EXCEPT IN THE LIGHT OF EVOLUTION."

So, from EP's perspective, how do uninformed consumers using the evolutionary old S1 part of their brain behave and make decisions?

The title of Geoffrey Miller's opening chapter was "Darwin goes to the mall." Miller breaks down products and services in the marketplace into 3 categories:

i) Practical: survival commodities (food, shelter etc.).

ii) Pleasure premium: private vices (mainly intimate pleasures).

iii) Display: which includes everything else.

It is in the display category where we most often find consumers making subconscious decisions due to the lack of motivation and ability to process the information about the product or the service, hence, using an evolutionary old part of the brain to instinctively display a trait about themselves. Where EP gets immensely interesting is in its ability to unearth insights into what humans instinctively aspire to display.

So, my friend has recently bought himself an expensive fancy sports car, a Porsche Carrera 911. When he took me for a ride in it with him, I was personally disappointed with how uncomfortable the seats were and how basic the overall interior was.

. However, as my friend suggested, you never buy a sports car for comfort or beautiful interior, you buy it for the superior driving performance and the experience it gives you. As he was driving me, I realized that my friend was a bad driver who was uncomfortable with speeding and he was extra wary about the speeding cars driving around him; mind you we were driving on a big highway, and the cars around us were only driving as per the speed limit, a fact that made my friend move into the right lane of the highway. As I asked him what he knew about what made this particular car functionally superior, the only answer he had was around the fact that he heard that it accelerates from zero to 100 km/h in 3.9 seconds. Observing his driving skills, this man was never going to use this one and only feature he knew about this expensive car he just bought. Obviously, he was using the S1 part of his brain when he made this particular purchase decision, i.e., it was a subconscious decision driven by a deeper, more instinctive, and primal urge. To give you a bit of a background, my friend is a highly educated, super successful business man whose business decisions have helped him establish his own business, he is in no way an ignorant man who often makes such primitive purchase decisions.

He is the same man who managed to self-teach himself his company's entire IT requirements, and with absolutely no IT background, managed to save his company hundreds of thousands of dollars in IT requirements. When it came to spending money on his company's IT requirements, he was highly motivated to process the information, and while he was incapable to do so, he self-taught himself to do it. When it came to buying a car, the same person was less motivated, less capable of processing much simpler information and ended up making his decision based on instinctive and primitive drivers.

Towards the end of our awkward drive, my friend conducted another irrational behavior, he offered to lend me the car for two weeks for no money, just as a favor for me to enjoy it for a bit. Another bit of more background on this man, he is known for how careful he is with his money (to the extent that some may call him cheap), and how uncomfortable he is with people using his stuff. At the moment it made no sense to me what drove such a decision, it was yet another irrational decision that I assumed is most probably based on another set of instinctive and primitive drivers. Well, EP helped understand such drivers later on.

EP's understanding of what drives consumers stems from Darwin's drivers for humans' behaviors, again, as a result of natural selection and/or sexual selection, DARWIN'S 4 DRIVERS FOR HUMAN BEHAVIORS:

i) SURVIVAL (NATURAL SELECTION): Avoiding predators, deter rivals, and find food

ii) REPRODUCTION (SEXUAL SELECTION): Competing to attract a potential mating partner

iii) KIN SELECTION: Impressing parents and investing in family members

iv) RECIPROCITY: Building non-kin alliances and friendships (e.g. via gift giving)

Charles Darwin

Based on the above drivers, Geoffrey Miller links cues that people find evoking in advertising to those they find evoking in human nature. Miller defines these "fitness cues" as features within our environment that can increase our "fitness opportunities" (such as our chances of survival and/or reproduction) - and that instinct entices us to be on the lookout for these cues. In advertising, this would translate into identifying cues in messages that play on people's instinctive needs. For reproduction, this would have to do with one's ability to attract mates; taking the place of the large, symmetrical, colorful, costly, awkward, high-maintenance, hard-to-fake fitness indicator of the peacock tail would be the large-engine, symmetrical, colorful, costly, awkward, and high-maintenance Porsche Carrera 911 my friend bought in today's culture. When it comes to the survival instinct, one's ability to deter rivals, mainly with big horns and loud viscous roars in nature, would, in today's mostly social, financial, and emotional rivalries, depend upon factors such as the followers on Instagram or Twitter (a factor that explains all the irrational behaviors we can observe on these two platforms), or an expensive flashy watch to signal out one's financial status to their social rivals. If we go back to my friend's purchase decision, turns out his evolutionary drivers could have been either survival by signaling out his success to his rivals, reproduction by signaling out his ability to acquire resources to a potential mating partner, or kin selection to impress his parents.

Oh! and the reason why he offered to lend me his car for two weeks was "reciprocity." While the above may sound too theoretical, we have actual scientific experiments proving that the purchase of a luxury sports car along with the act of cruising around in it are based on one of the aforementioned meta drivers, well, in this instance it is mainly driven by sexual selection. Such behaviors have their origins in nature before they existed in our modern-day marketplace, in nature, the two main behaviors that are the result of sexual selection are labeled or symbolized by the "peacock tail" and "lekking."

i) THE PEACOCK TAIL:

In an attempt to attract their female counterparts, male peacocks present their tails to display their attractiveness. This display goes against the theory of natural selection, since the tail also attracts predators, putting the males in danger of being hunted. Still, the need to attract a sexual partner is apparently worth the risk.

ii) LEKKING:

According to John E. Lycett and Robin I. M. Dunbar of the Center for Economic Learning and Social Evolution, "In nature, a lek is a communal mating area where males gather to engage in flamboyant courtship displays, and females stroll by to judge the performers and presumably choose the fittest, most resourceful or most amusing of the lot." Again, this explains why males are willing to put their money (showcasing their ability to acquire resources), health (showcasing their fitness, i.e., their good genes) or their lives in danger in order to attract a sexual partner.

If we take a look at one of Professor Gad Saad's scientific researches, one that was mainly around researching how hormones affect consumers and also how consuming can affect hormones, in both sexes. For example, the fact that when men drive Porsches, their testosterone levels go up. For starters, as previously mentioned, Saad draws a clear parallel between the peacock tail and buying a flashy, but he also draws a parallel between a man cruising in that same car along the streets of a busy downtown area while women around the area observe to Lekking in nature. To test some of his theories, Saad and a graduate student of his at the time, Jon Vongas, designed an experiment where they had men driving either an expensive Porsche or beat-up Toyota station wagon in both Montreal's crowded downtown and on a relatively empty highway and then measured their testosterone levels after each drive.

They predicted that (i) driving a Porches while women were observing will have the men's T levels go up, (ii) this will not be the case driving the beat-up Toyota station, and (iii) it will not be true for driving the Porsche on an empty highway. Well, their first two predictions were true, however, the 3rd one turned out to be wrong. In fact, driving a Porsche raised male hormone levels in men significantly in either environment. The conclusion was that it was not only that when men sense that women are reacting or observing them sending such signals, but that it is such an innate evolutionary driver that you do not even need observers around you.

There is even some evidence that driving a Porsche (or, presumably, some other expensive sports car) affects peoples' perceptions of men's height and likelihood that they will be philanderers. That evidence is reinforced by a study performed by Michael Dunn and Robert Searle in the UK. They tested how driving a luxury automobile affects how attractive the driver is perceived to be by others.

They took photos of a man and a woman of equal attractiveness sitting behind the wheels of a Bentley Continental GT and a Ford Fiesta ST. Male and female test subjects were then asked to rate the attractiveness of the drivers.

Dunn and Searle found that while women's rating of men's appearance went up when they were in the Bentley, men apparently don't care what kind of car a woman drives, at least when evaluating her for her looks.

WOMEN'S RATING OF MEN'S APPEARANCE WENT UP WHEN THEY WERE IN THE BENTLEY, MEN APPARENTLY DIDN'T CARE WHAT KIND OF CAR A WOMAN DRIVES

This takes us back to sexual selection and differences between genders in terms of what they feel they need to display or signal out to attract a member of the opposite sex. Men disproportionately feel the need to display their ability to acquire resources, this explains the fact that fewer than one in 10 Ferrari buyers is a woman.

1 IN 10

FEWER THAN ONE IN 10 FERRARI BUYERS IS A WOMAN

The above explains one aspect of irrational purchase decisions - after all, an expensive, impractical car is one of the least logical purchases a person can make! But similar explanations can be made for almost all irrational purchase decisions, such as:

i) WHY DO WE PREFER SWEET AND FATTY FOOD:

There is a reason why we're easily tempted to consume fatty and sweet food. Given all the negative consequences of over-consuming such food items, we can definitely conclude that they are indeed irrational choices. In nature, the nutritional value such items had were crucial due to the fact that they have long enabled our ancestors to survive and reproduce, during historical eras such as the Pleistocene, meat was the most efficient form of receiving calories and protein, while foods that were sweet such as ripe fruit generally indicated high levels of nutrients. As such, our taste buds evolved to have preferences for such food. The overconsumption of such food and the negative consequences that it entails, is in no way caused by advertising. This is more related to regulations, abundance of it, pricing and over-all education. As Gad Saad puts it "Advertising can convince me to visit McDonald's instead of Burger King. But it cannot convince me to prefer grass juice more so than French fries."

11

UNHEALTHY DIETS ARE RESPONSIBLE FOR 11M PREVENTABLE DEATHS GLOBALLY PER YEAR. YET, PEOPLE KEEP INDULGING IN THIS IRRATIONAL BEHAVIOR

MILLION

ii) OVER–SPENDING ON BEAUTY PRODUCTS?

Research shows that it is not only men who are over-spending due to evolutionary drivers. In another study by Professor Gad Saad, and his doctoral student and co-author Eric Stenstrom, the consumption behavior of women was analyzed over a period of 35 days, and the study revealed that during the fertile phase of the menstrual cycle, women were keener and more susceptible to overspend on beauty products and clothing. Such behaviors had evolutionary drivers with traces from our ancestral times. As Saad explains, it was the innate need to reproduce that has long drove women to focus more on mating-related activities at the time where they had the highest prospect of conception, which naturally happens during the fertile phase of the menstrual cycle. These are the same evolutionary drivers that drive women to subconsciously, and irrationally, overspend on beauty products and clothes during such periods.

In conclusion, we have a good case building toward why consumers make irrational choices, and again, this is in no way the shortcoming of advertising. And now, we have another solid case on how it is our evolutionary and biological blueprints that are driving most of our irrational purchase decisions, not advertising. Yet, let us not deny the fact that advertising throughout the years have built the knowledge, the skills, and abilities to influence people's behavior (that is, of course, within the constraints of how much we can influence people's rational decisions and their irrational ones in the context of their evolutionary drivers), and it is our choice, as advertisers, to either use such influence for the good or for the bad.

HOW CAN ADVERTISING INFLUENCE BEHAVIOR FOR THE GOOD WHILE STILL DELIVERING ON ITS CLIENTS' BUSINESS AND FINANCIAL OBJECTIVES?

The answer to the question is in
the upcoming chapter.

CHAPTER V

AN OPTIMISTIC DEFINITION FOR ADVERTISING

"In between seeing the commercial and seeing the thing... I am happy, and that's all I want: tell me how great the thing is going to be."

—

Jerry Seinfeld

UPON ACCEPTING HIS HONORARY 2014
CLIO AWARD

So far, recent scientific fields, scholars, scientists, scientific experiments, and theories have helped me challenge Chomsky's definition of the prime task of the advertising industry. And while his definition was one of an extremely pessimistic and negative perspective of what's the worst an industry could be doing. My argument has been one of two folds; one is the reality that uninformed consumers will make irrational choices irrespective of advertising, and one is of an opposite perspective of a positively optimistic potential definition of the prime task of the advertising industry.

UNINFORMED CONSUMERS WILL MAKE IRRATIONAL CHOICES IRRESPECTIVE OF ADVERTISING.

I realize that one might feel that this opposite perspective is pushing it a notch with arguments like how advertising has potentially salvaged economies and marketplaces from collapsing. If you might have thought that I have been too optimistic toward the ad industry, well, think again! For in this chapter, I will be pushing the envelope a bit more to make an argument that advertising can also have the potential to play an essential role to ensure the well-being of the human race. Bear with me, for once again, such arguments will have roots in scientific fields and will be backed up by scientific research. So, let's explore how the advertising industry might have been playing an essential role in ensuring the well-being of the human race.

As he is known for his observational yet sarcastically critical comedy, Jerry Seinfeld, upon accepting his honorary 2014 Clio award (an annual award program that recognizes innovation and creative excellence in advertising, design, and communication) made an interesting, yet slightly negative, observation on the role advertising plays in people's lives. At that moment, the advertising industry thought they were honoring an established celebrity for his contribution to the industry; however, his reaction was yet another negatively pessimistic one on the advertising industry. Yes, he was accepting the award but he realized that, regardless of the context and/or audience, the almost only publicly approved perspective on advertising cannot be one that is strictly positive (hence, the dire need for the arguments made in this book). Now, if we look beyond all of Seinfeld's sarcasm and harsh critique of the industry with statements such as "I love advertising because I love lying" we can actually find some solid insights into the positive role advertising can play in people's lives, a role that can be defined as doing good for the wellbeing of the human race.

"I LOVE ADVERTISING BECAUSE I LOVE LYING"

JERRY SEINFELD

Seinfeld discussed how advertising paints an imaginary positive future of the anticipated experience when using a product, an anticipation that is often (if not always) far from the realized future experience. He stated: "in advertising everything is the way you wish it was, I don't care that it won't be like that when I actually get the product being advertised." He went on saying that: "because in between seeing the commercial and seeing the thing... I am happy, and that's all I want: tell me how great the thing is going to be." He concluded this statement with a definition of the human race as "hopeful species." I am unsure if he is actually aware of all the scientific research and facts that back up his statements.

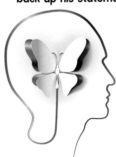

ARE WE AS HUMANS
"HOPEFUL SPECIES"?

For instance, while he defined humans as "hopeful species" both neuroscience and social science advocate that humans are more optimistic than realistic. There is also scientific evidence in Seinfeld's statements on how people are happy to enjoy the process of anticipating how an experience will be as they wish for it to be, even if in reality their realized experience is below their expectations. Scientists call this Optimism Bias, and it is defined as: "the belief that the future will be much better than the past and present." Apparently, this could be found among every race, region, and socioeconomic bracket, well, apparently 80% of humans are in fact optimists, or to be more precise biasedly optimistic. It is as Samuel Johnson wrote, "the triumph of hope over experience."

80%

Based on several studies published in Nature Neuroscience, 80 percent of humans are in fact optimists.

Throughout our evolutionary history, we have developed this optimism bias as a survival technique. The optimism towards the future, with some bias towards one's own individual future is needed for our own basic survival, it is also needed for our own wellbeing and happiness. The lead scholar on the subject is Tali Sharot. In her book *The Optimism Bias: A Tour of the Irrationally Positive Brain*, Sharot argues that even if the better future humans optimistically and biasedly draw/imagine for themselves is frequently an illusion, optimism has apparent benefits in the present, research has shown that this hopeful thinking keeps the human mind at ease, it lowers stress and improves one's physical health. Optimism can go as far as helping humans fight fatal diseases, for example studies of cancer patients has shown that patients under the age of 60 who are pessimistic were more likely to die within eight months than non-pessimistic patients even when both had the same age and initial health status.

The origination of optimism bias takes us back to evolution, and more specifically, how our minds evolved to be able to travel in time, what is scientifically referred to as "mental time travel." As humans, we tend to take this ability for granted, yet, it has proven to be crucial for our survival.

Hopeful thinking

keeps the human mind at ease, lowers stress levels, and improves physical health.

For example, to be able to survive in times of food scarcity, we needed to develop the ability to mentally time travel in order to foresee such a future and plan ahead for it, by saving food. Yet, with such mental ability came the cognitive awareness of our own mortality, the realization that at some point in the near or far future death will come and all of this will end, a realization that should have put an end to evolution.

An irrational optimism bias needed to evolve for humans to go on striving to survive and reproduce. The geneticists, Ajit Varki and Danny Brower, have discussed this in their book *Denial: Self-Deception, False Beliefs, and the Origins of the Human Mind*, arguing that there would have only been one way for mentally conscious time travel to co-exist with the awareness of mortality and that is through the evolution of irrational optimism bias.

Why continue to fight for survival and reproduction if all of this is eventually coming to an end?

THERE WOULD HAVE ONLY BEEN ONE WAY FOR MENTAL TIME TRAVEL TO CO-EXIST WITH THE AWARENESS OF MORTALITY: THROUGH THE EVOLUTION OF AN IRRATIONAL OPTIMISM BIAS.

Further research has shown that being accurate about anticipating your future leads to mild depression: Tali Sharot along with her colleague the neuroscientist Elizabeth Phelps, have conducted several research studies using tools such as functional magnetic resonance imaging (fMRI) to record the brain's activities as their volunteers attempted to imagine events that could occur to them in the future. According to Shalot, "the studies revealed that while healthy people expect the future to be slightly better than it ends up being, people with severe depression tend to be pessimistically biased: they expect things to be worse than they end up being. People with mild depression are relatively accurate when predicting future events. They see the world as it is." She goes on to conclude: "in the absence of a neural mechanism that generates unrealistic optimism, it is possible all humans would be mildly depressed."

Now according to the above conclusion by Sharot, within the context of the marketplace, where people are often in the process of buying products and services, we can conclude that without advertising (i.e., without creative, original, entertaining, and engaging communication, messages and experiences that give people an optimistic outlook toward their future, toward a future where they will look, feel, and act better than they do today) all humans might end up being mildly depressed.

Remember, we are more often talking about uninformed consumers, using their innate biological blueprints to make their purchase decisions. Yes, they are driven by Darwin's meta drivers, and while in nature the decisions driven by these drivers were to ensure survival and re-production, the same applies to the marketplace; they purchase a product and/or a service in anticipation of a future where they can comfortably and happily survive and re-produce. If they cannot imagine or anticipate a better future, then they are subject to suffer from a mild depression, if not of a severe one.

This does not call for advertising to actually lie to people, however, it calls for advertising to purposefully showcase an optimistic glimpse of people's future when buying and using the advertised product or service. An ad should be the brand and its users on their very best day. Research shows that people already have somewhat an optimistic outlook toward their future, adverting should creatively bring to life this same exact optimism, with the addition of a role for the brand to play in the future of people.

For instance, when one travels on Turkish Airlines, they are not expecting to see Kobe Bryant competing with Lionel Messi, however, this sheer moment of optimism such an ad brings to people could actually improve their wellbeing at the moment of watching the ad while they imagine themselves traveling, even if one is to fly on the Airlines to realize that in reality, the competition is in fact among two crying babies competing on who can cry the loudest.

The optimism an airline ad provides could improve its viewers wellbeing by helping them imagine themselves traveling – even if, in reality, on any airline, it will not be Kobe and Messi competing, but a group of crying babies.

If you think that giving advertising the role of helping people with their wellbeing in the present is already pushing it with this positive perspective, well, guess what!? Advertising can also potentially alter people's future for the better. Neuroscientist Sara Bengtsson, conducted an experiment in which she manipulated positive and negative expectations of students while they were about to be tested, she has done so while scanning their brains. Now in order to encourage expectations of success, she pumped up college students with encouraging sentiments/compliments such as smart, intelligent, and clever just before having them conduct the test. To put other students down and have them feel negative toward how they will perform, she used words like stupid and ignorant. Apparently the students performed better after being pumped up and complimented with affirmative messages. As she has scanned their brains' activities, she found that the students' brains responded differently to the mistakes they made depending on whether they were complimented with words like smart or put down with words like stupid. When a student made a mistake that was followed by positive words, she observed enhanced activity in the anterior medial part of the prefrontal cortex (a region that is involved in self-reflection and recollection). However, when the participants were put down with the word stupid, there was no heightened activity after a wrong answer.

It appeared that after being put down with the word stupid, the brain expected to do poorly and did not show signs of surprise or conflict when it made an error.

When a student who had just been complimented made a mistake, she observed enhanced activity in the anterior medial part of the prefrontal cortex, a region involved in self-reflection and recollection.

Such affirmative and complimentary messages are often used in advertising, and this is another role advertising can potentially play in people's lives. As the research has shown, when you tell people that they will be smarter, look better, feel more confident; you very often put them in a mindset that can actually help them attain a better future.

When Nike tells someone they can perform better at a sport, when Apple tells someone they can be more creative, when Always gives girls in their early adulthood empowering messages, when Axe tells a guy he can get that girl, and/or when Johnny Walker asks people to "Keep Walking"; very often such advertising can alter the future of these individuals for the better (proof points of such case studies will be discussed in the next chapter).

Real-life case studies on the positive impact of advertising:

1. DOVE

REALITY: a study with 3,000 women in 10 different countries revealed that only 2 percent of women believed that they are beautiful

THE AD: an on-going campaign with encouraging and motivational messages inviting women to confidently embrace their natural beauty

RESULTS: 71% of the women who interacted with Dove's positive ads felt more beautiful

71% of the women who interacted with Dove's positive messages felt more beautiful

2. NIKE:

REALITY: an unrealistic definition of performing well at sports has been discouraging the average individual from physical activities

THE AD: "find your greatness" was an open invitation for anyone with a body to aspire to train and work-out as an athlete

RESULTS: a 55% increase in Nike+ memberships, proving that more average individuals were encouraged to work-out just like athletes

3. ALWAYS:

REALITY: as girls hit puberty, they are exposed to early womanhood's cultural and societal pressures and stereotypes. Such factors causes their self-esteem levels to drastically drop, while the same happens to boys, the drop for girls is twice as much, and what's even worse is that data shows that men's self-esteem rises higher than it was pre-puberty, yet, it's the opposite case for women.

THE AD: a challenge to the cultural stereotype to what it means to do something "like a girl", while the stereotype puts a certain label on it, the ad proves that to do something "like a girl" means to just do it like anyone else

RESULTS: almost 70% of women and 60% of men stated that watching the ad changed their perception of the phrase "like a girl"

4. AXE:

REALITY: in Turkey, the general cultural stereotype is that real men should not be apologetic, hence the notion that men do not apologize

THE AD: Axe, the deodorant brand, wanted to fight this stereotype by integrating its ad with a popular local TV series that has long encouraged this specific stereotype

RESULTS: in just 30 minutes, 3,750 apology messages were shared on Twitter by Turkish men

Turns out men do apologize after all

The aforementioned proof points are in no way the actual potential basic definition of the prime task of the adverting industry, it is a positive twist to showcase that when devised properly, positively and purposefully; advertising can help people draw a more optimistic outlook towards their future, and as we have seen, several research studies have proven that such an outlook is needed for people's wellbeing in the present. Such an optimistic outlook can also help them and encourage them to alter their future for the better. Therefore, as stated earlier, in a world mostly dominated by a marketplace making the majority of our daily decisions around what we are about to purchase, and given the fact that more often we are neither motivated nor capable to process the information on our purchase decision, then we can possibly conclude that without advertising all humans can potentially be mildly depressed, they might not be able to live up to their full potential and advertising is in fact needed for the wellbeing of the human race. In this world with all the aforementioned transactions between sellers and buyers, sellers have been pushed to change the approach they have been using to transact with their consumers, and consumers' expectations of sellers (and their brands) have also been changing, this change is simply articulated by the notion that sellers need to build brands with a human purpose.

The definition of a human brand purpose, its effects on the business of sellers, the lives of consumers and the overall economy is to be discussed in the upcoming chapter.

CHAPTER VI

CORPORATIONS DON'T GO TO HELL AND BRANDS DON'T GO TO HEAVEN

"To me, marketing is about values. This is a very complicated world. It's a very noisy world... Our customers want to know who is Apple and what we stand for."

—

$\mathcal{S}$teve $\mathcal{J}$obs

H IN
V VoLU

As we have seen earlier in Chapter 2, the birth of the very first, yet basic, form of mass advertising and brand building came as a reaction to the first industrial revolution. Today, we are embarking on what is being referred to as the fourth industrial revolution (4IR), and with it, comes the need for advertising to adapt and cater to all the peculiarities of this recent revolution. This chapter discusses a new wave of relatively new form of brand building and advertising thinking that has also been playing a positive role for markets, communities, and humans.

THE FOURTH
INDUSTRIAL
REVOLUTION

4IR is driven by digital technologies, connectivity, and disruptive innovations that has already altered many well-established industries. Think hospitality and Airbnb, transportation and Uber, retail and Amazon or Alibaba, TV and Netflix etc.... the same alteration has been happening to marketing, advertising, and brand building. Consumers have never been more connected, and have never had more options on offer.

This means that with predictive algorithms (along with personalization and recommendation engines) advertisers can constantly ensure that consumers are receiving their personalized message along with their customized offer. Yet, before we get too excited about these capabilities, let's take a step back and acknowledge how annoying and noisy this can become.

Imagine that this mass consumerization on digital platforms initially started by offering two options of a product or a service, this then jumped up to 10 options, and now up to an astonishing 1,000 options customized to every identified consumer segment. Yes, as an industry we got too excited about what we can do with these new capabilities and forgot that we are often connecting with consumers who lead busy lives, lacking the motivation and/or ability to process our 'personalized' message, consequently using S1 part of their brain, meaning that they are behaving instinctively and irrationally, and regardless of how much we managed to know about them. If they do not know our brand and share positive feelings of love and trust towards the brand along with the message we are putting out there for them, we are just being noisy, interruptive, and annoying. Hence, more and more of these impulsive consumers are opting-out by unsubscribing, unfollowing, un-installing, and simply disconnecting away from brands (according to statista. com, in 2019, roughly 25.8 percent of internet users were proactively going out of their way to block advertising on their connected devices).

Today's consumers are being bombarded with two extreme ends of sellers attempting to connect with them. On one end, there is the greedy corporation that is only after their money, and on the other end there is the deceivingly selfless brand that is pretending to only care about their wellbeing, as if it is not being funded by a business that needs to be profitable. Well, since the reality is that greedy corporations do not go to hell and selfless brands do not go to heaven, in the 4IR, it is going to be the middle ground here on earth where advertising can potentially play a more positive role.

25.8% 25.8 percent of internet users proactively went out of their way to block advertising on their connected devices

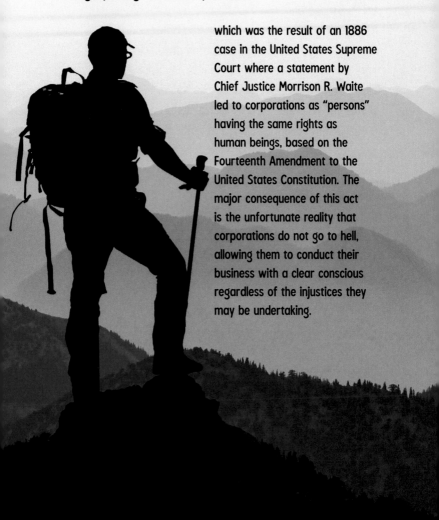

The 2005 the book The Corporation: The Pathological Pursuit of Profit and Power shed light into how the legal system has given birth to corporations with the entitlement to most of the legal rights of a person. The common theme in the book is how corporations are legally being treated as persons, which was the result of an 1886 case in the United States Supreme Court where a statement by Chief Justice Morrison R. Waite led to corporations as "persons" having the same rights as human beings, based on the Fourteenth Amendment to the United States Constitution. The major consequence of this act is the unfortunate reality that corporations do not go to hell, allowing them to conduct their business with a clear conscious regardless of the injustices they may be undertaking.

Well, as discussed earlier, this is one side of the argument, and the other side is in the fact that brands do not go to heaven as a consequence of them conducting selfless charitable deeds. However, here on earth there is a middle-ground with work that help build the brand and give back to their audiences and their communities. This is done by anchoring brands with a human purpose and bringing this purpose to life through purposeful activities.

The need for brands to be anchored by a human purpose is a relatively recent business concept that has proven to produce increased profits, revenue, and overall value to business organizations. For a brand to thrive in today's increasingly busy world with uninformed consumers impulsively choosing to opt-out, it needs to justify its existence in people's lives. A brand purpose is built on a specific point of view about the world we live in. It has beliefs, attitudes, a tone, a personality, and, most importantly, a mission. It identifies a real source of tension affecting people's behavior and is committed to resolving it.

Today's consumer, that same consumer who decided to opt-out of brands' activities, are more willing to conduct business with brands who have clearly revealed their human purpose. For instance, according to Accenture Strategy's Oct. 2018 Global Consumer Pulse Research (with 29,530 end-consumers in 35 countries) nearly two-thirds (63%) of consumers prefer to purchase products and services from companies that stand for a purpose that reflects their own values and beliefs. At the same time, Kantar Consulting's report "Purpose 2020", which used data collected from a multitude of surveys from around 20,000 marketing professionals and 100 interviews, revealed that purpose-led brands had their brand valuation increase by 175 percent over the past 12 years, this is in comparison to an average growth of 86 percent. Also, Edelman's 2018 Earned Brand study has proven that nearly two-thirds (64 percent) of consumers around the world make purchases based on what a company stands for, an increase of 13 points since 2017. Finally, In May 2015, Unilever stated that its "brands with purpose" were growing at twice the speed of others in its portfolio.

However, this relatively recent concept about brand building has also been immensely misunderstood, where we see businesses and scholars confusing it with the concept of brands selflessly being charitable to their communities. First and foremost, a brand purpose is set to help the business, yes, it is about the human side of the business, and how the brand and the business can play a more meaningful role in people's lives, but let us not confuse this role with purely selfless acts.

Brands, be it through their CSR activities and/or through their brand building activities, should realize the difference between the two aforementioned acts and charity and/or corporate philanthropy. CSR and brand building should always make business sense. As per Michal Porter's framework on "CSR as Strategy" they should be within the intersection of the inside-out (how the business and/or the brand is affecting the society and/or the target audiences) and the outside-in (how the society and/or the target audiences are affecting the business and/or the brand). It should be a win-win situation for all parties. So hypothetically speaking, if you are a bank operating in a country with an agenda to nationalize the workforce (the outside-in) and your brand purpose is about helping people realize their dreams (the inside-out) then it only makes sense that your brand building activities are around upskilling the local workforce, regardless of how tempting it may be to proactively initiate an effort to help people lose weight, and how many awards such an act may help you win.

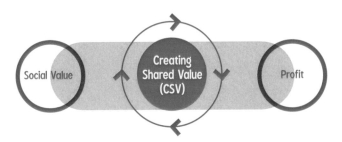

Michael Porter's CSV

Again, brands do not go to heaven, brands help uniformed consumers see the human side to a business and help the business build a human relationship with its consumers. It is a bad thing that corporations do not go to hell, while they enjoy the legal entitlement of humans, at the same time there is the other reality that brands do not go to heaven, while they are the human side of a business.

The thought here is not to preach for brands not to do good deeds, it is preaching for brands to stay true to their business and the target audiences they are serving. In the same manner that CSR needs to make sense from a business ROI perspective, brand building activities need to also make sense from an ROI perspective. A human purpose and the initiatives to bring it to life is a long-term commitment by the business, accordingly, it needs to be sustainable for that same business. It can neither be a gimmick for the brand to pretentiously be part of a currently popular conversation, nor for the brand to win some creative award. If a business executive is tempted to help a human cause, that happens to be irrelevant to his brand's human purpose,

well, spending his shareholders' money on it will neither help him go to heaven (it's not his money after all) nor will it help the business. And since brands do not go to heaven, it is not helping the brand.

To ensure that the funding of such purposeful human activities by brands are sustainable, and at the same time are actually positively impactful for humans and communities, we need to be realistic on what it ought to be, and clearly acknowledge that it makes business sense. This is done when brand builders precisely define human tensions affecting the lives of the consumers that the brand is attempting to target along with the relative role that specific brand can play in order to aspire to resolve these tensions. While such thoughts are more often aspirational than literal, let's not forget people's optimism bias and how in the case where these tensions are not fully resolved, advertising can still ensure the wellbeing of people in the present and alter their futures for the positive.

Regardless of how irrationally instinctive uninformed consumers are being, they are still humans seeking to buy into a brand with cues they want to signal out about themselves. This goes beyond a feature the product allows them to utilize, again, we are talking with uninformed consumers making irrational choices. They seek brands with aligned moral values, aligned beliefs and views about the world.

There's one extreme that is pushing this into charitable deeds, and while this is great on the short-term, it is unsustainable for the business of the brand. The middle ground is work that feeds into the monetary equity of the brand, yet, at the same time gives back to the consumers of the brand.

If we go back to the 4IR, and all the data and personalization capabilities it has equipped advertisers with, we will realize the decisions we need to make. Do we ignore the fact that uninformed consumers are seeking deeper instinctive cues about the brands they are about to use and just use data to hammer on practically rational personalized messages? Or do we use deeper human insights by marrying the same sources of data with human psychological analysis to unearth tensions the brand can aspire to resolve for people? Well, to find the answer let us take the hypothetical case of a dinner party where you are the guy with intentions of approaching a woman you find attractive, and your objective is to get introduced to her and take her number. Keeping in mind that from her perspective, before giving you her number,

she is still going to be missing perfect information about you (i.e., uninformed), and regardless of how smart and logical she may be in assessing you as a potential partner, her decision, at least at that introductory stage, is going to be somewhat an irrational one.

Now, imagine that, as our modern-day advertisers, you are equipped with real-time data on the lady, along with the ability to customize your message and proposition for her. So, using the same mechanisms that modern day advertisers are using (for instance, populating over 1,000 personalized option) you approach the girl with information such as noticing that she was having her drink at the pace of one sip every 8 minutes, and now that she has been missing her drink for 10 minutes and 30 seconds, you acknowledged her need for a new drink and your proposal is to cater to her need with a new drink (while she neither realizes the need for a new drink nor does she know how you collected a piece of info about her that she does not consciously possess).

In addition, now that you knew she wanted a drink your gesture could be perceived as cute and attentive, but your data tells much more than the simple fact that she is overdue for a drink, you also know exactly what wine, and what year, and where she usually has them, and recommend which other wines she would love, as well as other places close to her residence and work or even where her friends hang out (I know this sounds creepy, however, believe or not brands have been doing all this).

And now you are expecting her to be delighted about your proposal, that is without attempting to evoke any emotional response from her toward you, and without revealing much about yourself (other than the fact that you freakishly know so much about her behavior). Well, unfortunately, had this been the case then we would have seen more data analysts (with genuine intentions) hooking up with beautiful women than we see it with men who have a more instinctively genuine approach. And while there isn't a one-size-fits-all guidebook on approaching a potential partner, it is universally known that revealing one's intentions (i.e., human purpose) and attempting to evoke an emotional response based on deeper human insights about the target is a much more effective method than simply collecting data to repeatedly (and annoyingly) personalize a message that does not necessarily cater to any human insight.

The same is applicable to the context of the marketplace, where the man can be the brand and the woman can be the potential customer, a context where brands are faced with the decision to have a genuine approach revealing their purpose and attempting to evoke an emotional response based on a deeper human insight, or use real-time data analysis to hammer messages that people are not completely comprehending the reasoning behind them being targeted with this specific message, along with the fact that they are yet to emotionally relate to the brand.

According to Tim Stock and Marie Lena Tupot in their AdMap article "Cultural Mapping," big data and digital analysis produces uninspired consumer profiles. Data today is available in a number of seductively enticing forms, and brands are lured into a false sense of security, thinking they know exactly where to go and how to get there. What seems to be missing in all this, however, is the human element that may be neglected in the focused pursuit of neat answers from extensive data analytics.

Yes, people are communicating and are extending their reach globally through the amazing tools of technology, but they cannot be defined by technology. The authors state "People are the manufactories of cultural meaning,

To get closer to the lives of real people and understand the context they inhabit means dedicating time to thinking and analysis. Answers do not live in databases. They live fueled by contextual knowledge and confident intuition.

This is in no way a black or white kind of decision, it is not a decision to either abandon data to only do purpose driven communication. There is a middle ground to bring the purpose to life and use data to help both people and the brand. The DMA Feb 2018 Data Privacy Report showed that while 78% of people feel that brands are benefiting from their data in a disproportionate magnitude, yet, the very same people are willing to share their data if this act provides them with tangible benefits.

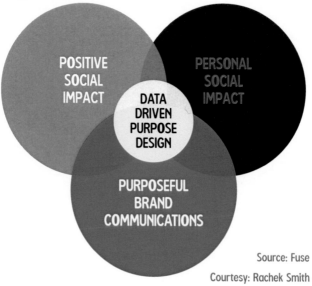

Source: Fuse

Courtesy: Rachek Smith

Data can and ought to be used as a force for the brand to deliver on more purpose-driven activities, however, this fact does not seem to be on any major agenda, for instance, the Bloomberg's Data for Good Exchange, has taken out any brand building or purpose driven activity from its agenda and/or program.

The reality is that brands will continue to rely on personal data and consumers will continue to expect more purpose driven brands and purpose driven activities, it is in the middle-ground between the two where both will find more long-term benefits. On the bigger scale, it's the application of the framework "good for business, good for consumer, good for society."

In practice, we have seen a long list of brands across various industries utilize data to develop more effective purpose-driven activities. One example would be Bumble, a dating app anchored by a human purpose. As part of activating its purpose, Bumble used personal data and customized algorithms to stop misogyny on the app. They first used data to identify the aforementioned tension points that their brand can help resolve, that data showed that 42% of women experienced negative contact on dating apps while the reported crimes triggered by dating apps was increasing by almost sevenfold during the last two years.

Then they also used data to activate their purpose, they basically blocked and deactivated the accounts of users whose data revealed that they were using foul and/or harassing language.

Then there's Axe targeting men, using data to unearth deeper human tensions facing these men and activating their brand purpose to resolve these tensions; while ensuring that such activities benefit both the consumer and the business. Through partnering with Google Search, they were able to identify the social pressure facing men and have an immediate answer to attempt to resolve this pressure. Data showed that "is it **OK** for guys to…" was one of the most commonly used search terms on Google by guys, a term mostly associated with the pressures men face while trying to not be perceived as less manly. Accordingly, Axe launched their 'Is it **OK**' campaign. The campaign resulted in a %25 increase in purchase intent and %34 increase in positive sentiment in global sales while reaching 4bn global impressions.

| is it ok for guys to e | Q |

is it ok for guys to experiment with other guys
is it ok for guys to experiment
is it ok for guys to eat edamame
is it ok for guys to eat tofu

—

Source: Axe: Is it ok for guys

Today, advertising as an industry has an opportunity to both positively contribute to humanity and to our clients' business, and we have seen many examples and scientific evidence of our potential to achieve all this. Yet often in reality, we have been passively submitting to any negative definition of what we do, consequently, we have not been able to clearly define our prime task ourselves, and this is why in the greedy pursuit of being more efficient and more effective in the short-term, we have been blindly jumping on the bandwagon of any recent technology, regardless of how gimmicky it may be, while not caring that we are being interruptive, noisy, and annoying. This is neither helping humans nor the business of our clients. We have neglected our potential positive contribution to economies, societies, and humans, and to do so, we should not let our prime task be defined by someone else other than us. We should define this prime task and consistently ensure that we are living up to it. The attempt to have such a definition of the prime task of the advertising industry will be discussed in the upcoming chapter.

CHAPTER VII

DEFINING ADVERTISING: THE PRIME TASK OF AN EVER-CHANGING INDUSTRY

"I regard a great ad as the most beautiful thing in the world."

—

Leo Burnett

As I was writing this book, I would often take a step back and wonder, "Am I deceiving myself here? Am I using scientific evidence simply to defend my own job?" But, despite my hesitations, I remained convinced that by shedding light on the industry's potential impact, we could redefine its prime task and encourage advertisers to pursue a more positive purpose.

I was also encouraged by the thought that if we admen were to simply succumb to the notion that what we do for a living is wicked, we would only cause severe harm - not only to the industry, but to entire economies and the overall wellbeing of the human race. After all, the advertising sector employs around 1.9 million people; we couldn?t possibly all be evil. And given the fact that the average person is exposed to around 5,000 ads per day, and that, at only 36 months old, an American child recognizes up to 100 logos , it is safe to conclude that our work has become an integral and impactful part of people?s everyday lives.

The average person is exposed to around

5,000 ADS

per day. There's no doubt that the ad industry is among the most impactful industries on people's lives.

The need for businesses to advertise and build their brands isn't going anywhere. But our industry is facing a challenging time, not only due to its image problem but also because of substitute services from adjacent industries tapping into our livelihoods, clients struggling to find value in our offerings, talent being charmed into other industries, and holding companies hesitating to invest in their ad agencies. Today more than ever, a more affirmative definition of the ad industry's main task is needed - a definition that will optimistically sum up the realities of what the industry can achieve, instead of hinder and dismiss advertising by describing it as an effort "to ensure uniformed consumers make irrational choices."

So, if Chomsky's definition misses the mark, what is advertising's true role in society? Let's take a look back at the industry's positive potential, breaking it down into the four folds we previously covered:

1/4

The ad
industry is
critical to
economies.

¼) The ad industry is critical for economies

As we have seen, the market theories upon which our economies were built are subject to major assumptions and hypotheses that have made them inapplicable in reality. Key among these blind spots is the impact of information asymmetry. The ad industry itself is a product of our economic systems, and while we can debate how functional or dysfunctional these systems may be, no one can deny their immense contribution to human development. Given the inapplicability of the market theories that most marketplaces follow, the advertising industry is needed to strategically equip sellers with trusted and beloved brands. At the same time, the industry plays a vital role in creatively connecting these brands with consumers to positively reassure them about their purchase decisions, irrespective of how uninformed such choices might be. This ensures that buyers are happy to pay the full price for their items, and sellers can afford to sell high-quality products and services instead of defective ones.

---

4 This figure is based on neuro-marketing studies by Dr. Allen Kanner at the Wright Institute in Berkley, California. Although the studies were on American children, the same could also be assumed for children from other countries.

As we can see, without advertising and brand building, buyers and sellers alike would be pushed to settle for low-quality products, potentially putting our economic systems on a crash course toward failure.

THE ADVERTISING EFFECT:

BECAUSE OF ADVERTISING...

1. Buyers are happily willing to pay the full price of what they are buying

2. Sellers can afford to sell good quality products & services instead of defected ones

3. And the economy is salvaged

Therefore, the first fold for the definition of the objective of the ad industry can be the following:

¼

"A prime task of the advertising industry is to help sustain our economic systems by allowing sellers to offer their highest quality products/services and ensuring that buyers willingly pay the full, proportionate price."

2/4

Advertising is
needed to help
humans survive
and reproduce.

²/4) Advertising is needed to help humans survive and reproduce

Throughout these pages, we've discussed scientific facts and evidence detailing how people make marketplace decisions. Considering information asymmetry, along with the fact that people often lack the motivation and ability to process information about the product or service they are about to buy, purchase decisions are almost always made impulsively. This information is typically processed through the peripheral route to the brain, using the instinctive and intuitive S1 region of the brain. Such decision making is based on a biological blueprint that evolved through cycles of natural and sexual selection. It follows that, when people make such purchase decisions, they are looking for "fitness cues" indicating whether a product or service will help them survive or reproduce, and there is a clear link between the cues people might find evoking in advertising and those they find evoking in nature.

For reproduction, this would have to do with one's ability to attract mates - from the flamboyant peacock tail to the attention-grabbing foreign car. When it comes to the survival instinct, in nature, one's ability to deter rivals hinges mainly on big horns and loud viscous roars. In today's world of humans, where rivalries depend more on financial and social status, cues can be found in flashy watches and the number of social media followers - and we interpret these signals through brand attributes and advertising cues.

Nature vs. Marketplace

For reproduction, taking the place of the peacock tale in nature; are brands like the Carrera 911 in today's marketplace

Nature vs. Marketplace

For survival, taking the place of a viscous roar in nature; are number of followers, friends, mentions and likes on social media

Humans aren't limited to using shiny luxury items in order to project their desired image. For example, an entrepreneur with a tech startup might signal their status by walking into an office wearing flip flops. Commenting on her business attire, Pilar Stella, cofounder and managing partner of the tech startup Alchemy P4 Fund, said, "I'd call my style a mix between sassy startup founder and pixie surfer mermaid unicorn. Sometimes people don't get me - I think that is part of the journey as an entrepreneur."

These simplified examples may seem strictly superficial, but consumers rely on these cues when presented with a wide range of choices because it would be too stressful and time-consuming to sort through the information about all of the alternatives. Which option is healthier for you and your family? Which will signal that you are the right candidate for the job? Which will help make your parents proud of you? Which will show your partner that you are committed? Advertising and brand building clearly make this decision-driven world an easier and less stressful place to navigate.

The average grocery store has
40,000 to 50,000 choices

Looking back at the animal kingdom, it's clear that there could be nothing more natural than relying on fitness cues in the decision-making process. In his TED Talk "We're All in Marketing: What Evolution Tells Us About Advertising," Ethan Decker gives the example of the male elk, which must grow huge antlers made of bone, weighing 40 pounds in only three months - how inconvenient and irrational? But that's the price they need to pay to signal their superior genes to the opposite sex.

———

In an attempt to attract females, male Elks grow 40 pound antlers made of bone in only 3 months.

Even flowers are a form of advertising. Many plants reproduce through a process called pollination, in which they must attract animals, known as pollinators, to carry pollen between flowers. Accordingly, flowers' beautiful colors are just their way of signaling to pollinators that they have the best nectar and pollen, which the pollinators need for nutrition. Insects and other creatures unintentionally carry pollen from one flower to the next as they are drawn to the next promising-looking meal. In today's world, these signals are found in brand attributes and advertising cues.

Pollination

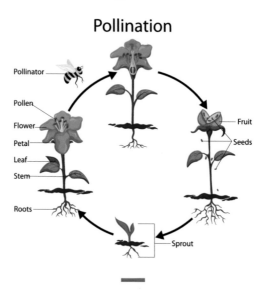

Flowers are a form of advertising for plants to attract potential pollinators.

As Decker put it, "We aren't superficial creatures, we are symbolic ones."

"WE AREN'T SUPERFICIAL CREATURES,
WE ARE SYMBOLIC ONES".
—
Ethan Decker

Yes, there are extreme scenarios where advertising takes advantage of such irrational decision making, but in no way should this be the definition of what the industry does on a whole. On the contrary, it should be defined as follows:

²/4)

"A prime task of the advertising industry is to help people joyfully and easily navigate the marketplace by allowing them to find cues in products and services linked to their ability to survive and/or reproduce."

3/4

Advertising has
the potential to
ensure the wellbeing
of the human race.

¾) Advertising has the potential to ensure the wellbeing of the human race.

I'll be the first to admit that my thoughts on the industry's potential positive impact often go too far - yes, I have claimed that the ad industry can potentially play an essential role in ensuring the wellbeing of the human race. Yet, I cannot claim this without the disclaimer that these very same skillsets are often used to take advantage of people's need to pursue happiness. Such an act is labeled as "affective conditioning," meaning that, in the instance where people lack the motivation and ability to process functional information about the quality of a product, advertisers can deceive them by associating the product with generic positive elements (think linking detergent with greenery and generic beautiful scenery). Such acts have proven to be very effective, with scientific experiments showing that people who have undergone affective conditioning would choose a product 70 to 80% of the time when it is paired with other positive elements.

---

[5] (a pen in an experiment by Melanie Dempsey and Andrew Mitchell.)

Again, every industry and every profession can suffer from experts taking advantage of such human vulnerabilities; yet, it would be reductive to define these industries by such acts. On the contrary, we should aim to identify the positive potential of these industries and professions, and encourage its members to pursue these meaningful goals.

IF ADVERTISING IS ABLE TO MAKE PEOPLE HAPPY, THEN ADVERTISING CAN POTENTIALLY MAKE PEOPLE BETTER PROBLEM SOLVERS

20% Happy people solve nearly 20 percent more word puzzles than unhappy people

The same is true for advertising. If, as neuroscientist Mark Jung-Beeman has shown, "happy people solve nearly 20 percent more word puzzles than unhappy people," advertising's ability to bring people joy can potentially make them better problem solvers. Recalling Tali Sharot and Elizabeth Phelps' fMRI studies proving that optimism bias is essential for the prevention of mild depression, we can conclude that advertising's ability to allow people to foresee a more optimistic future for themselves plays a role in ensuring our wellbeing and protecting us from despair.

If advertising can allow people to foresee a more optimistic future for themselves, , then advertising can potentially ensure our wellbeing and protect us from despair.

IF ADVERTISING CAN MOTIVATE US TO ALTER OUR FUTURE FOR THE BETTER, WITH STUDIES SHOWING THAT SUCH ENCOURAGING MESSAGES HELP HUMANS ACTUALLY PERFORM BETTER, THEN ADVERTISING CAN POTENTIALLY HELP PUT PEOPLE IN THE MINDSET TO IMPROVE THEIR LIVES.

If advertising can motivate us to alter our future for the better, then advertising can potentially help put people in the mindset that can allow them to alter their future for the better.

If advertising can motivate us to alter our future for the better, with studies showing that such encouraging messages help humans actually perform better, then advertising can potentially help put people in the mindset to improve their lives. With these facts, another prime task of the advertising industry can be summarized as such:

3/4)

"A prime task of the advertising industry is to help people lead better lives and live up to their potential by contributing to their happiness, helping them feel more optimistic about their future, and giving them the confidence to perform better."

4/4

Advertising helps businesses, people, and communities mutually thrive in the Fourth Industrial Revolution.

The Fourth Industrial Revolution brings with it the rise of the super connected. In their pursuit of short-term profits, most businesses are excessively using data and personalization to stalk and interrupt their consumers, repetitively getting in their faces. Consequently, a growing number of people have been proactively blocking advertising from their lives; in fact, according to Digital Information World, 47 percent of global internet users used an ad-blocker in 2019). Creative advertising and long-standing efforts to establish a trust-based connection between buyers and brands have taken a back seat, allowing data-driven personalization to take over.

However, we know how buyers make their decisions; we know the deeply instinctive needs they are usually trying to fulfill when purchasing a certain brand. So, we also know that data-driven approaches are often far from helping brands fulfill such human instinctive needs. Here, there is a huge opportunity for advertising and brand building to again play a positive role for businesses, society,and people.

Research shows that a major element of the aforementioned "instinctive needs" surrounds people's search for brands whose values are aligned with the values they aspire to demonstrate in themselves. It's around the larger role the brand aims to play in their lives - the human purpose of the brand. Advertising and brand-building are critical to establishing such connections between brands and the public.

Advertising connects businesses
with people by establishing a set
of mutual human values

When coupled with a genuine understanding of human behavior, data can help us unearth deeper insights into human tensions people might be facing (remember Axe and the pressure of masculinity, Always and young girls' confidence, and Nike and the definition of greatness). Ad men can encourage businesses to connect with people by revealing and activating their brand's human purpose. Instead of utilizing data and personalization to annoy and interrupt, they can be used to establish genuine human connections that benefit people, communities, and clients.

BRAND	HUMAN TENSIONS THE BRAND RESOLVES:
AXE	PRESSURES OF MASCULINITY
BUMBLE	MISOGYNY
ALWAYS	YOUNG GIRLS' CONFIDENCE DROP
NIKE	UNREALISTIC DEFINITION OF GREATNESS
DOVE	REAL BEAUTY

Accordingly, a fourth potential definition of advertising can be the following:

$^4/4)$

"A prime task of the advertising industry is to ensure that marketplace transactions benefit people, businesses, and society. The advertising industry does so by giving brands a human purpose to resolve relevant and meaningful human tensions of their target audience, not only encouraging people to buy the brand but also encouraging businesses to give back to their communities."

***

CONCLUSION

***

Is there a single "prime task" for the complex and sprawling advertising industry? Chomsky would say it is to promote irrational behavior. Our clients would perhaps say it is to sell their products. But neither statements come close to the whole truth. In fact, I don't believe it is possible to boil the entire industry down into a single, comprehensive definition - that's why I've provided four, and there's certainly many more that would be equally acceptable!

Like every commercial or creative pursuit, advertising can be a double-edged sword, and its drawbacks have made it a convenient scapegoat for a wide range of societal ills. With tremendous respect to Dr. Chomsky (and the many other intellectuals who disapprove of our work), advertising doesn't exist to disturb or upend the natural order - nor do human beings need to be pushed into making the countless irrational, uninformed decisions that mark our day-to-day life.

In Leo Burnett's mind, a great ad is

"THEMOSTBEAUTIFULTHINGINTHE WORLD",

and I find myself agreeing with his assessment. It can serve as a reflection of human nature at its most pure - our deepest desires, our humor, or our optimism for a better tomorrow. A great ad informs, entertains, and inspires. It gives us a shared language through which we can relate to each other, and transforms something as ordinary as a pair of shoes into a new means for self-expression.

For 10, 30, or 60 seconds at a time, advertising can transport us to an alternate reality, and challenge us to discover something new and exciting that has been lurking within us all along. I can think of no more practical and rational way to spend a minute or so of my time. And it is a pleasure, privilege, and responsibility to be a part of the industry that makes these magical moments possible.